Disability

DOES NOT MEAN

Stupidity

Disability

DOES NOT MEAN

Stupidity

A Collection of Poems and Quotes

SHANNIQUE SMITH

| ISBN: | Softcover | 978-1-6641-1790-7 |
| | eBook | 978-1-6641-1789-1 |

Print information available on the last page.

Rev. date: 10/06/2022

To order additional copies of this book, contact:
Xlibris
UK TFN: 0800 0148620 (Toll Free inside the UK)
UK Local: (02) 0369 56328 (+44 20 3695 6328 from outside the UK)
www.Xlibrispublishing.co.uk
Orders@Xlibrispublishing.co.uk
844127

Contents

Use words like a paintbrush to create effective results.

My name is Shannique Smith. I was born 24 March 1993. Writing is like another bone attached to my body which enables me to function in a world where you often feel lost in a misty daze. Our minds are so powerful, but we often refuse to let doors be unlocked in our pathway to find inner answers.

It is weird that I am writing a book. I learnt to read and write at age twelve. I attended special need schools growing up. I am blind in my right eye and have limited vision remaining in my left. I did not want to learn. I saw no point in doing so. Childhood grief was all I knew. Teachers thought I was dyslexic, but I was not. I was dealing with internal issues which took time for me to grasp.

I was born in Jamaica and came to the UK when I was eight years old. My father went to the USA, when I was four weeks old, and my mother came to the UK when I was five years old. My parents did their best during their absence. I on the other hand just felt alone and out of touch with humans.

I was born with congenital bilateral glaucoma. It took six weeks after my birth for doctors to realize I had this condition. Life in Jamaica was hard. I was born into severe poverty. I underwent a number of operations from six weeks old. I was on medication which was expensive that my mother could not always find money for. Hence the reason why she came to the UK to seek a better life. At the time I did not understand this at all. I just felt left behind when she went. Both parents living abroad, I felt neglected. I was put in boarding school. On holidays my grandmother would pick me up.

My grandmother was my everything and when my mother took me to the UK once she was more settled, I wanted to go where my grandmother was. I cried every day to return to the one person who was my life.

The pattern of sorrow followed me into my education. I would go to school, but I never took in what the teachers were teaching. When I was eleven years old in year six, all my peers were doing their SATS where it would determine which groups they would be placed in upon arriving at secondary school. I did not do my SATS because I could not read or write. Shameful yes, children were horrible beyond words.

I overcome my battles by pushing forward. It was already bad that I had a visual impairment. Not being able to read and write, I did not want that label too. I proved the special educational system completely wrong. The moment I learnt to read and write, I was taken off aeroplane mode.

I wrote my first poem at the age of twelve. I knew at that point I had a talent for writing. My first poem was published in a book. At fourteen I won a poetry competition that over 3000 students took part in from different schools within the borough, where I attended school. I got the opportunity to perform my winning poem on stage in-front of over 500 people.

It was a bizarre time. There I was at fourteen reciting a poem on stage that I had written...I entered the doors to secondary school, unable to read or write and here I was talking in front of a crowd.

I received A in my GCSE English literature. No one thought this would ever be the case at all. I had a winning energy. Reading gave me strength; reading was my therapy. When my English teacher was reading my coursework essay on Hamlet written by William Shakespeare. She was astonished at my analytical skills.

My relationship with education became bittersweet. I would start courses then drop out of the course. At nineteen years old I enrolled on an access course in Business Management. I decided, I wanted to go university to do a degree in business management. I applied to five Universities, and I was given an offer from all five.

I have ventured into various areas. I have written for magazines, newspapers, websites, I was a media ambassador for my local borough, I have worked as a fashion stylist, I have, experience in working in Human Resource as well as Marketing. I obtained a degree in Human Resource Management.

The journey has been draining. I have stages of severe depression. Sometimes I am doing exceedingly well, other times the zip of depression sweeps in.
Life is hard that much I know. I am trapped in my thoughts often. The struggle is a battery control of reference leading to regrets. I refuse to stay still for a long duration, I am not that character.

Writing a book have been a accomplishment I wanted to see come alive. I needed to have enough life experience before I took on such a heavy task. I officially started to enquire about getting a book published. At a period in my life where earth appeared to be at a standstill.

I honestly thought the world was at its very end in 2020. The whole system was numb. We were machines being told what to do, where to go because no one was certain where the coronavirus disease would take us. Power was completely lost, lives were taken. Tears of many falling on our bodies other than in the morgue.

First and foremost, I would like to give a big thank you to all persons along my journey who have helped me.

Disability

Disability is looked at like the circus of society. Acceptance is the burning strain.

To have a physical or hidden disability is a problem. A physical disability, it is on display playing, over and over again like a TV show. No one chooses to be disabled. The inadequacy to do certain things for yourself and sometimes nothing at all.

Depending on where you live in the world. You know, you have to be more tough. You start off like a snake, continuously shedding skins to adopt to the environment or else in the bin you go. To form into your own version of uniqueness. A unfavorable request similar to playing a game of chest.

Societal pressures make us feel, you can walk tall like a giraffe. Where the world tells you. You are not welcomed in our raft.

Fully able-bodied folks say we are all disabled. They are not the ones being perceived like a piece of distasteful work, rather than a Picasso painting; therefore, they should not be commenting. You do not know, how we feel. As you get older, doubts whistle far past just the freckles of horror.

Emotional growth is a must, without it you are spinning with the wind and will not be missed.

Faults are found with disabilities. Living should not be the life of us. You do not have to do anything, towards an outsider for them to make you feel bad about the baggage. You eagerly wish you can drop off like a load full of terror.

Alternatively, the system looks at us like we should be far more thankful. When all you feel is a sense of abandonment instead of a precious piece of treasure.

Lifelong partners is what most crave for. Well, when you have a disability, the inability is extreme to find anyone in the stream. You are not expected to have choices, no matter who comes our way, we should go with them by being grateful someone has looked in our direction. You don't know if they are with you for love or out of pity. A voice is not a weapon we should hold. Instead, we are the objects of tools for psychological torture.

The media have given comfort somewhat, to let unaware people with this unspoken stigma, know they are not alone. You can be held captive or become a real warrior.

Lost

Lost, the need to belong is like a rivulet.
The river flows, a soft sound reflects a union of melody. The river moves along, water drains at the beginning of the river, it looks still as it grinds with laughter.

The liquid does not stay still. The rhythm dance in a party of chaos. Lost is the river as more and more, H2o is taken to build structure.

A shovel is raised in an area, to cover the sinking damp. No amount of digging can lose focus of the hole which is lost completely in a camp.

Lost is the Kimberly Diamond Mine in South Africa. Once the hunting ground, to get diamonds. Currently all that remains is a huge dent, all of which was caused through the ruins left from participants, molding a nation further into severe repercussions.
Lost is the cloud, polluting the airways to breathe confined by data.

Quotes

Self-pity stops success.

Outer beauty is gold inner beauty is platinum.

Love is like a rope. It can either kill you or save you!

Behind the skin there should still be a character.

The mind is like a mansion.

Success is like an engine which have the power to travel.

Humans should be like shoes.

Emotional pain is a part of your life journey. What is not okay is to allow this to happen repeatedly. This will not make a complete you!

Depression is like a deadly weapon and if not destroyed early can cause long life implications!

An outer achievement is not so powerful as an inner self one. Outside forces can decay whereas an inward one is instilled.

Ambition is sexy!

GPS should be the Oil ring controlling batteries in a circle.

The worst trait, humans have is when they let others get inside their head. Having mental power of your own is game changing that way you set your own mental trend!

Nature has amazing strive of power. Anse Source D'Argent in Seychelles illustrates this. One of the most alluring beaches on earth. What makes this beach so unique is the natural occurrence leaving behind granite boulders.

The moment, you do not have human respect for a person, just leave them alone. Do not talk badly about them or to them.

Capture good moments like a picture instilled in your mind.

Whenever a person does you wrong, do not seek revenge, life will deal with them.

Folding away pain is not a good fix. Healing needs a clear shelve!

You are the engine of your car!

When you hurt the person, you love, it is like acid been poured on the skin.

The truth is the truth, but someone else's truth is not for you to tell, that is their story.

To be held mentally is way better, than to be held physically. Minds twirling together to form complete answers.

Bitterness, if not handled well will walk in the wrong pathway with you in life.

I put my mental health first! I close the world out at times. A lot of humans do not understand it, but I do. I know the mental pathway that I have travelled through.

The wrestler is the sheets biting away frustration.

Nuclear power plant is the humble base for an efficient breakthrough.

I take refuge in writing. The words that I write are my teardrops.

Emotionally damaged is like a never-ending forest fire.

The feeling of being trapped in your thoughts. Looking for some way out but you cannot see any.

Photos, speak to you but it's up to us as individuals to talk back.

A bullet is the signal for a change of control.

Turn off the tap please! Drip, drip, and drip my thoughts are flowing over.

When you feel you are not loved, you start to self-destruct!

A cave wave is a thunder whereby demon's flow.

The ability to unlock the mind is a pressures gift which very few people have.

Look at me but try not to judge because you were nowhere near, when I needed someone!

Real bodies with imperfections, add value to ownership to your property.

Graphite have been crafted in pens for centuries. It is now an emerging trend leading to graphene.

Despair is the permission to let go.

Life is hard but what is even harder is dealing with regret, knowing very little has been accomplished.

Loyalty is like a tree. It takes time to grow and seasonal changes is certain.

Disability is the distance mile many run from.

Energy is happiness and anger is the fire that stops that energy from lighting.

Beauty remains when things are left unspoken.

The journey to acceptance will be a scribble but you will find your way through.

Separation from civilization is not always bad. You can grasp your own flow of thoughts quicker.

A tunnel with holes looking ahead is the Benagil Sea Cave Beach in Portugal. It greatly represents the need to keep protecting faith. Bigger inside than what it displays outside.

Men have built immoral bridges but also bridges creating a great deal of fortune. The holocaust and a coal mine represent just this. Overburdened Conveyor Bridge F60. Boarding between Poland and Germany. Both countries at one point were in great deal of distress. Now the coal mines creating a region to be rich far passing all sorrows.

Confidence will lead you to a safer place internally.

Labels given to individuals is like a blueprint.

Be super secretive that way, only you have the power to walk away from unanswered questions…

Sorry is like a chair. Once all balance giveaway then you pull for it.

More people would be loyal, but no one want to feel that heart wrenching pain of betrayal.

Life lessons will have you feeling you are in a mental cave but it is up-to you to search for the light.
Do good in life towards others. Guilt will have you in deep regret if you do not.

Emotional pain is like a volcano awaiting to erupt if not dealt with properly.

Eyes, have the power to unlock answers that speech cannot.

It is best, to start like a flawed line in a painting but finish off the added element to the room.

Being overly conceited is unattractive. It is like leaving a toilet seat up when it should be placed down.

When you are left alone in silence with your thoughts, hidden problems arrive.

We are compasses waiting for directions.

Being sensitive is like a screen with barcodes you will break easily.

I remember when I was seventeen years old. I was boarding a plane from London Heathrow heading to JFK New York. Upon boarding my name was called as I need special assistance whenever I travel abroad. I was walking on the passenger boarding bridge. I had two staff members standing on both sides of me. When finally reaching the aircraft the male staff member said, "There is a step-in front." I do not shy away from admitting I need help.

The feeling of being damaged, makes you feel like your heart has been fractured, you start existing rather than living.

I gave you access to my body, not my powerful mind.

Climate change is the ink to a harmful signature.

Being sneaky is like wearing an uncomfortable jumper. It will leave you with rashes.

The prisoner was memories of not leaving the cell.

It is a struggle when you do not understand your own destiny. It is like you are in a developing room; waiting for pictures to print.

The transporter should be your future, knowing time is the space craft.

Two things in this world are certain heartbreak and tears.

I learnt to read at age 12. Teachers thought I was dyslexic, but I was Just an angry child, not willing to learn battling childhood issues. I started to write poems. I then realized. I had the talent to draw with my words.

Be happy, when no one takes your side, that way you know you are alone and not worrying about chapter changes.

I am not to be used. I am not a piece of recycled item.

Statues can lead to metaphorical meanings. Diminish and Ascend by David Mccracken in Australia. Does just this the steps start off big but the further upwards you go; it gets smaller with a closed door at the top. This is like reaching an end of a movement.

In my darkest mental cave moments, I have answered a lot of unresolved questions internally.

Grief has no expiration date. Events replay in our head all the time.

A look of admiration lets you know there is hope ahead.

It is not selfish to protect your heart. What is selfish is allowing yourself to be used.

The life contract that we feel will be fair is not.

Shelter is the base station worthy of cords not to be entered by predators.

The ancient Romans were the sanitizers to worldwide growth.

Revenge is the sinkhole collapsing a system full of doubt.

Time moves differently when you are actively pursuing an end goal.

It is pointless reflecting back and wishing, you could change things. The best thing to do is move forward with a different note.

It is fine, for people not to understand you, as long as you understand yourself. You are the person having to deal with worries presented.

There is no flawed way of living. There are flawed moments.

The lighthouse is the broom sweeping the dust of a transfixed view.

Body shape is the illusion craving to cultural shock.

The chilling effect is where two people are attracted To one another. They talk with their eyes now this is couture designed to be unwrapped.

Fast charging is the net trapping wounds to the unknown.

A balcony attached to a house is like a hair comb building to style a frame.

When you feel your heart has been broken, you wish for an end to intervene.

We often do not evolve with our significant other. Instead, we drift apart.

It takes far more energy, to be angry than what it does to be happy.

You must firstly be desired by peace instead of growth.

I have been stared at my whole life. I guess, I must be an impressionable exhibition.

Finding inner peace is hard, when you have a disability, but it can happen. To be different is difficult in the beginning however in the end you are much more aware of life dimensions.

Words change rooms, actions change bridges.

I carry my handbags, the same way I carry life with strength.

The fraudulent activity is the network. Taking wealth from countries without control.

Unresolved childhood MISERY will follow you into adulthood and will either be a stop light which can turn red or green.

There is no bad enemy, it is just the opposite side you need to win against.

Jealousy is the music felt by most.

Take a moment, to rebuild what was lost but gather your thoughts first and then act.

The best beauty is one that not every individual can see physically.

Do not dumb yourself down to let someone else elevate.

The sunglasses protect you from the sun but nothing will protect you from pain.

You can be the driver or the passenger the choice is ultimately yours.

As humans, as we get older, our physical beauty may fade but our mental beauty as we age is powerful.

Help others with knowledge, you have gained. You will be changing their outlook in the end.

Do not be jealous of someone else. Your building is not finished being built just be patient. You will love the finish.

It is truly a blessing, when there is a room full of females, who own their beauty without intimidating one another.

Physical beauty alone will not save you. Be that person who is full of knowledge!

Society is the glowing enterprise declining generation wealth.

Violence is the cutting-edge causing PTSD.

When two persons are deeply attracted to each other, it is an electronic shock.

The systematic world is not always kind to humans with a physical disability.

Do not tell someone how to feel. Everyone has their own thought process.

There are some fun moments which are pointless redoing. Just remember it, for what it was.

Magnet is the instrument keeping areas off the world together, one of which is ITER. International thermonuclear experimental reactor. The most dominant man-made magnet on planet earth. This is crazy because the earth core brings its own magnetic field. A symbolic meaning as humans can outrank natural forces.

California is one of the most lost places on earth. Death Valley where heat kills passing souls. Fences crossing into another country territory but the saddest one is Skid Row.

Hell can be earth. Valley Of Death in Russia and Lake Nyos in Cameroon mirrors just this. Both places picturesque have volcanos with poisonous gas. Taking many lives.

Give a preview of yourself not the full movie.

The grade is the graduate, falling to graffiti scattered on walls needing cleaning.

Laziness gets you nowhere. It is like an artist with a paintbrush and a canvas but no pictures being painted.

Love is a swing, it pushes you backwards and forwards.

If you do or say something which is wrong and you feel bad, then you are not that character.

It's amazing, how we cry more about the pain inflicted by others, more than what is self-inflicted.

The moment you let go is the moment cords will be adjusted.

When a smile is shared so uniquely, there is a bond not to be broken.

Life is like a photo shoot. The fixation for perfection is the main shot.

We continue, to evolve with technology but not so much with our inner self.

My vision is not good, but my hearing is full of success. My hearing is super great, I can unlock pin numbers.

I have entered the lottery games online. Played over four hundred times and won small amounts of money. I have now come to the realization that the best lottery prize worth over £70,000,000 is my mind.

It is better to be misunderstood by others than to be controlled by them.
I have learnt that my disability means living with style aura.

I am not for that. I am not about to sit in pity for long. I have off moments that is for sure but doing so will not solve the problem. I walk with my head held high, dressed up with my handbag in my right arm and my perfume you can smell from a distance.

Be the unusual barbie that way a copy cannot be imitated.

The feeling of nostalgia can be like a ripe fruit or a thunder; causing the fruit to fall even though not properly ripe.

Titanic and Avatar. Are two of the most memorable films with an intriguing storyline which is released 12 years apart. It takes time for a story to develop. Just give yourself time to grow, you will fall deeply in-love with the end results.

A bad Reputation is like a phone call, ringing in a displeasing tone.

Not blinking will hinder the stages.

The refusal for a forever narrative.

A poem and a painting are two of the most heartfelt instruments in the world.

You must first be a true friend to yourself, before you can be to anyone else.

Who feels it knows it. Humans are endlessly intuitive.

The only gangster which is needed is strong will power to keep moving.

You can start a fresh...your mistakes are yours to deal with no one else. Society often make you feel that your mistakes mean the end of you which is far from the truth.

Educate yourself about various topics, that is a killer weapon of knowledge.

The writer has no effective words without experience and the artist is nothing without the view.

Being polite, will make you look more presentable.

If the biggest organ on the human body is the skin. Then why do humans disfigure it greatly.

Body image is environmental more than what it is psychological.

When an event first happens, it feels like it has been magnified but as time goes on. All you see is the horizontal line.

Some of the most intelligent people, have been crafted in society.

Social media can be either an excellent teacher or the biggest betrayer. The little bit of sanity, I have left I refuse to make it skate away.

Emotional wealth is diamond. You must dig through the gutters to reach.

Stephen Hawkins and Alison Lapper. Have both lifted a mirror of strengths by not giving up no matter what it took.

Take control of your sexual health. Be loyal to yourself because you will be the one living with an incurable disaster.

Low self-esteem is like a bucket awaiting, to be filled with toxic waste.

Observe the frequency of blessings.

The strain is not walking with the power of forgiveness.

A twin flame is rare to find. Once you find it hold tight.

Go with someone who challenges you. Little growth is made with a steady pace.

The mint is the forging machines refreshing industries.

A necklace is like humans. One person will know that person, who knows the following person and so on.

We are living in a ring far beyond the solar system. Technology is the circle pointing upwards the Dyson Sphere proves just this.

Percentages is the weighing variables.

The worst days. Will lead to a better understanding.

Giving away your ideas before lift off is like going to the airport, without your passport. This hinders you from travelling.

Peer pressure will be a gamble you will regret.

Diction is my craving. I have no mercy for the keyboard.

A dam will be a harsh chemical taking lives.

Covid-19 will never be fully dislodged.

Perceptions will be a swivel gun that can cause horror.

The trap is believing we have not become biodegradable to envy.

The definition of a real hot girl. She is someone with swag turned all the way up with intelligence, a physical flow like no other.

The ocean gives unity to peace.

Never let the person, who tried to see you in bandages let you melt away to nothing.

Humans can be heart-wrenching blizzards.

I was disappointed with life for a long time. I Found myself sinking deeper and deeper into hatefulness.

Fine beauty gives off a spark.

What I want does not transfer to what is happening.

A mental theft outweighs a physical theft.

I remember when I was fifteen years old. I was going through a transition-I found it hard to accept the fact that I have a sight problem. A teacher told me to look at my glass as half full rather than empty. One year later that same teacher found out she has glaucoma. It was then she understood what I was feeling.

The same way your phone can die if not charged you will die too.

Your skin is a project.

A follower destroy lives a leader inspire it.

To be silent is to be cold not being visible is frosty. Melting away in misery hidden behind curtains of sorrow awaiting to repair with hope.

We are yet still battling with our future selves. Hoping for what could be. The uncertain which can leave you empty.

Physical beauty is not worth much if not consisted of a profound intelligence.
Love...the very word has many bearings. The feeling if bonded to another person will have you in a mist. A tiny part of you like a raindrop keeping you alive.

Strength is the stairs, and the wall is the laziness to keep you down.

Physical things do not move me. A profound mind keeps me.

The crazy part is her confidence is heavy now this is something trendy.

Sometimes the stranger is ourselves.

A mental breakdown equals opportunity for discovery.

Naivety is like a rusty belt, needing to be unbuckled and thrown away.

Contour your talents.

It has been a self-recovery mission.

You will breathe again. Your breath is only temporarily paused.

The best trigger to pull is curiosity.

I have been mentally, unpacking unpleasant memories to create understanding.

It has taken for me to go into a bin of regret to change.

Being insensitive will not shield the hurt.

The code is simple healing is necessary.

Being Judgmental is like being homeless.

Closure often means rewinding.
The trap is the feeding ground to lose sight of communities without financial literacy.

Actions are a wire which can shock others.

Waves from the sea are extreme fear.

Help is like a zinc. It can help build you or leave you with a scar.

Being blunt is the election freely subsiding feelings.

Prayer is the void many ask for no more.

Changes are like microbes. You cannot always see the effects. Unless a outbreak amplify.

Languages can be the mistaken union.

Coat

Coat is like a school. The education given is the protection to guide you but that is not the full armour, to rescue you.

Teachers are the syllabus. Pointing where to sit with the drones you need to fetch.
To regurgitate information fed which should be succinct. We are taught to get education. It will break all the travelling barriers.

Your brain is the train to run but you should study the line ahead, to be completely aware of all the channels to overcome.
You are taught about atoms, but this is only partial.

Diction, the way in which language is used, recycled just like a square root. The fixation with Equal Rights stems from lack of emotional intelligence. The wide majority have 206 bones in the human body but there is still a lack of inclusion. Thomas Hardy discussed in his novel Tess of d'Urbervilles, periodic situations a theme routinely with a bad crown.

The stages are coincidentally a myth. It is a winter of heavy blizzard. Before you can even put on the coat; you must look around and ask why success comes with a frown.

A coat is an expensive piece of fabric. Not easy to switch that must be why, they teach us about the stock market and the great wall of China. Thinking one day, we too will soon get rich. By learning all the geographical areas to cover, to help with the trip ahead, to stop you from surrendering no matter the weather.

The window

The window is the eyes for the room. It has been said that "Faith is the key that opens all doors" will the window be that and so much more.

The curtains are pulled back. The mesh behind stares at attention, letting you know that the sun is preparing to shine. The lenses are lazy.

A haze to the heart. There is no point in clearing the sledge of the window. The sledge is the block to stand on, to look through the window.

The window is the device, the soul you need to break free. The tale to be told for passing ears. Only you can tell no one else.
The curtains are the blanket of misdeeds needing forgiveness. Forgiveness is only possible if strength is implemented. The external breeze has left the window with knowledge it can command all surface.

The window is the microphone, volume on mute. Tension speeding through the speakers as all it wants is not misunderstood.

A connected friend

A connected friend. We are often slaves to our thoughts. I was a refugee full with heavy doubts. The summer sun introduced us.

We saw each other briefly the year before. I was with anger the stranger was peace. We spoke properly on the steps of your front porch for hours the year after.

Conversation flows between us. There are no boundaries to our topics. A miracle which led me to be forgiving to extreme thinking. I can share which no one can intervene and tear.

If we were to carry out the unimaginable, greatness would come alive. In moments of distraught, you were the connected friend to remind me how far I have reached, and hard times does not spare any drought.

To have an escape route is to have moved from one coast to the next. Searching for missile in different corners. Distance tricks our thinking.

To be heated is deadly. I did not accept myself, but you did. You understood the smoke-filled air around me. I just wanted out of the blaze.

Regret has little place if sympathy is applied, to move forward. Be like a gate but a visible one with holes, others can see but still need to get close enough, to gain access to enable entry.

You have been that gate awaiting to be opened. You brought me first gift of self-recovery.

The Elevator

The elevator, the doors are slowly closing. Seven individuals are standing still. The button is pressed.

Two of the seven individuals' eyes greet one another, locked like a pillow to a case. It maybe hoods love. Where they fight hard for today and deal with tomorrow's results. Physical attraction is the core.

The pair, who's eyes are locked temporarily one of them has an issue. There is a physical flaw on one side of her face. She tries her best to look in the opposite direction, but it is too late for that. He notices already what she is so desperately keen to hide.

He looks at her, all he sees is a rare form of beauty. He looks even further into the detail presented. He is the examiner giving the grade, but she is unaware. No one else matters to them both. In those few minutes they are flying away from the elevator. To a place where no Judgement the maker, beauty is the shaking craft that glitters all known.

She has no idea, what is going on, she has feelings of separation. to her, he is just another unwanted guest. She decides to let him in for those few seconds.
Before separating, he gave a whisper of goodbye, by letting her know you are perfectly framed.

Aeroplane

Rows are announced, to let you know who board should. One can feel as if they are attending a graduation.

All expected customers have the same motivation. To reach a particular moment of freedom full of joy.

Lift off is approaching the wings like a bird, circles in motion to take off. The traveler carries cargo like the Antony AN-225 MRIYA. The biggest aeroplane in the world originating from Russia. MRIYA which means dream in Ukrainian, but no wish has been made but a nightmare that will not go away.
Before fully leaving the ground. A lesson about should a catastrophe occur is shown but sadly, not even that can really save the ruined wires departing.

A sum of classes is the deciding factor, a weird infrastructure. For some riders this means a goodbye and others it is their first hello. This is not show and tell it simply hell.
No one likes this ride, it is unfair. In no way as straightforward as the periodic table. There is a chemical imbalance just like life.

All you can do is look to the stratosphere.
Classes are the shelter. The turbulence is the agony you want to stop moving. The fasten seat belt sign are turned on, right above your head this must be the therapist. Talking is not the solution at this junction.

The fallen hacker, to the sky that is the aeroplane. A member sits quietly in an aisle by the window. Hand holding their face. A small television is at the back of the seat in front. Pictures moving in a animated gesture. A cartoon is playing, preternatural because cartoons.

have been the root to real predictions. What is considered a mere thought is acting out with great confusion.

Neglect to oneself, for many years has led to this moment. GPT-3 one of the stars ahead. A form of artificial intelligence, the concept is to survey past behavior. Whereby finding a compound but it will be a while before it leaves any ground.

A few hours into the ten-hour air journey, tears of smoke let loose-a buildup of frustration has gone. Turning back is not the answer. For far too long that has been the sleeping mechanism. The pilot, voice echoes throughout the aeroplane, it is idiomatic the conclusion draws near; therefore, get ready to unfasten the seat belt without any fears.

The ghetto

The ghetto, it is an environment not for the weak. The hourglass figure is the talk of the streets. The hourglass can shift differently, if turned the correct angle. The captain of the ship controls the movement of the sand falling on the glass; therefore, you Just need to start and do not just fumble.

The defective buildings speak to the passengers. You can scrape the dust formed like a prisoner awaiting a visitor. The smell of urine in corners it lingers.

Most are here because they have no choice. A door with a roof is the priority but the bullets tell a completely different story. Pipes break frequently but there is hardly any money, to buy groceries, let alone to save up, knowing one day you can move, to a neighborhood with water not contaminated with flint. Shops are in close radius to each other. The mode is Black Lives Matter.

Little expectations are an umbrella. The rain of the past falls often on the avenue. A will was announced, you can interject the asset left behind or start to stretch to get the next.

Jealousy speaks, it is the capital which causes many thieves. This is something ironic because they too need a new AC, along with a pair of sheets.

A lace wig with frontal most ladies want. Aspiring to look identical to females on platforms Causing a frenzy as most hate their hair. This is not fair because they are left without edges. Hiding away like a government facility such as Pine Gap.

The AIDA model in desperate need. To raise awareness about threads showing on Instagram, interest to viewers all in a woe. Possible clients a desire to look a specific kind of way. Followed by actions breaking their accounts with the welfare checks now this is an illusion.

Young minds are the loading dock. Many are picking up a rock, now this is absolutely no surprise. A generation curst, maybe the reason why gentrification was introduced but is this really any use? An upgrade for a better life firstly begins deep inside of you.

Relationship

A relationship, the conquest is the most intriguing. A flirt with the person other than just staring at their shirt.

You question the eagerness steaming, to ask them out on an official date. Other than just remembering the scent of their perfume, each time they exit any room. The thought of a relationship, replaying a voice who sweeps away the mystery.

Contact is formed, a trade of numbers. The text messages follow then the call that beeps away, even when you are trying to sleep.

Three years and a half are great then it turns to, designing arrangements whereby disrespecting all retrospect.
Distance knocks heavy, while you question why the sudd
en change. You start to get apprehensive. The very thought leaves you empty.

Once you discover the meaning behind such a risk. Your stomach twist, your heart beats faster, tears drop. You ask them "Why didn't you just leave me, if you wanted out." You keep on thinking to yourself a total mockery has been made of me.

The worst part is all persons around you, knew what was going on. Not one of them gave you any hints. If it was the other way around. For certain they would all jump in. Selling you out faster than a pint of gin.

Personal attributes make no sense. You gave your heart. You presented yourself well, both physically and personally.

Healing takes time. You cut off all form of contact since January. A text message reaches you from them in mid-May. An addition of more apology is made. Auto correction cannot undo the heart wrenching pain.

If he told you to stop breathing, you would have done it before this strain.
There were other pursuers. Deep down they were not the one, who made your face smile with humor.

You thought you were better. All you did was hide what was the hidden agenda.

Second best is not the launch, you agree to receive. If you had done to him, what he has done to you. He would not even want, to have heard your name ever again. Outsiders say "Get over it, no man is faithful" a standard within most communities. Females are forced to put up with. Well, I for one withhold.

My feelings were not spared when you tried to damage my mental health.
It has been said that love is not meant to hurt. Then why is it a undesirable statement, to make you shut out all heavenly landscape.

How Can It Be

How can it be that we are living in a world of misery? The ecosystem appears to be cursed. An indignant spell has been put on planet earth.

We care so deeply about superficial things. That it took coved-19 happening for us to go to do more Google search.

We are on borrowed time, we are in a electronic fog, navigating towards the end. This was predicted way back in history with the help of a pen, where-one week would feel like a day. This is far past just a cosmetic trend.

How can it be where we are trapped by monetary policy? Where it dictates who eats, who die or quench their thirst. Inflation is the market we are all the products. Giving a service in a bubble which should just really burst. Like a crack between a floorboard, you can rest your fingers through.

How can it be, where we are ruled by technology? where the biggest headquarter is Silicon Valley.

We are all kings and queens but, our jewels have been Stolen. Slavery and the holocaust are two of the most deeper-rooted, bitter part about planet earth human memory. Where it shifted many Humans Rights away just like the tectonic plates. The thought alone will make you hate. This may be why the four corners of earth are in a state of nervous shock. To some it seems like a conspiracy, where around every 100 years we are faced with a deadly sickness that wakes.

How can it be where politics, stipulate the rules to tell us where to be in society this is beyond cruel. Now, where is the unity to give any form of a shape. A paradox of plenty, some of the countries in the G20 group are the ones feeling it the most. No, astonishment especially knowing that they were the invaders exchanging lives for a quick note. How can it be, where ageing is one of the biggest enemies? It is seen more of a sin, being committed than a luxury, to know that you have lived close to a century.

How can it be, where religion is like a cult, causing conflict? Rather than breaking stereotypes about preventing you, from being free demolishing the scars that caused a division.

Statistics, suggest there will soon be a shortage of food; yet there are plenty of guns. Every time a war occurs, we are all praying surely this will be the last one. Violence seems to be the only karma. Truth be told this only creates more uncertain drama.

Cancer, the shooting arrow which strikes, more chords than music at a symphony.
Drugs are the addiction of pleasure. Scoring more games than a basketball player playing pro, now who is the player.

How can it be, where animals share a code of loyalty that continues to be humans greatest tragedy.

Society

Society is like a tsunami awaiting to be anticipated. Abandoned is the grass that do not grow beyond Blood Falls. A spit of saliva narrows to the rails gripping a j-turn.

Grouped in various categories, like a batch of vanished demur, anxious for a twilight to appear.

The never-ending cycle of finding oneself in the wrong tank. value is the target but who is the leader of such a intel. The pivotal vinyl record calls.

Society is like a never-ending building because new parts are constantly being added. Judgement is the eyes of the pictures. Often it is dark but sometimes full of gleam. The radiation encrypted to let you know the living still need cleaning.

Social issues are repeatedly, the mix of negligence forming all frictions. An indecisive attitude towards authority, to make you ponder what does gratitude really signify when there is a switch causing envy.

Stairs

Stairs by the subway. One by one they creep further into a dim flame.

It is manmade. Not naturally clear like Son Doing Cavern in Vietnam. The biggest cave in the world. This will make you hover around.

The stairs are Foundation, to climb from like the soldiers, hiding from the opponent troops, yes this is really true.

The stairs are used, Brittle with the destruction of being worn. Shoes thrown on the face like a masked fully torn.

The stairs may come in a skin or skeleton. The skin is protected feather. To stop the stains from gathering. The skeleton is exposed. Showing the gaps in between trembling like Hussaini Hanging Bridge which is in Pakistan.

To climb from one end, to the next is a mission. An iron is dropped steam escapes. The dismay of the flay is set in motion.

The stairs creaks as one by one steps break away. Not made from acrylic hence the reason it will not melt and cheat.

A table positioned nearby. Mahogany to be exact but that is a hard wood. The stairs questions why it has not been destroyed and put in a sack. One foot of the table portrays hints of bites. Both items from the same family joining a pack to fight.

Used

Used, the feeling of being declined like a call made. Swap, for a need to satisfy one own purpose.

Used is the wrapper, which was wrapped up, neatly and suddenly thrown away. Dissolute is the feeling of gratification having the carriage to push, until no balance is made for the passenger.

Used is the brick thrown at your self-esteem, each time you feel calm but instead, greeted with recollection that have no escape strategy.

Used is the cycle to the race, to win but not many ever honestly will.

Used is the prototype. The experiment to work. An example is made to show it can be used.

A Token

A token is something so divine. Extraordinary to the eyes and ears to those who elicit in any way. Like a Wi-Fi connection.

A token is like freshly fallen snow. Snow unfreezing gathering all around. To fugitive mammals it peeks with rightfulness this is free flow.

The falling snow is still but only temporarily. Like cancel culture. Sticks are attached which are the veins to events, far too remarkable to grasp for one single episode.

A token such as the Salar De Uyuni that is in Bolivia. A view you would think is too magical to be real therefore it must be surreal. If it were to be described to you. It holds salt a vital mineral but the most catching bond is the world lithium.

A token a dimension like the ufo. Aliens are believed to be fictional. A blade heavier than in the games of thrones.

A Follower

A follower is someone, who lack their own inner direction.

It is best to be like a sword, pointing straight ahead. No looking sideways because forward thinking you are.

A follower is the bench of the park. They are not the tree that stands alone with a trunk-formulating its own reasons. Whereas the bench is made by another to be used by passing bystander.

The tree stands firm no matter the temperature. A bad forecast temperature change. Autumn is the season of change; a new way of survival is made. Summer comes new leaves are on the branches, most inner answers are answered.

A follower is the clothes peg, you use to hang the garment on the line. Easy to pull both sides to release.

A follower needs to feel part of a group. The need to feel established is the target. If not accepted the withdrawal symptoms take effect.

It may last for months or even years. Only rehab which are life lessons will heal the sickness.

Metamorphosis Of Hope

The look you gave of hope like a caterpillar about to turn into a butterfly, knowing change will appear soon. If eyes could seal the deal yours did.

The day we met was a drizzle. Sadness filled but with that drip of hope recovery could emerge. We are different but so very much the same. Literature is the eyeball of aspiration which was first highlighted.

There are two types of intelligence-you consist of both. There is trained intelligence where books teach you. Then there is inner intelligence this is where your own village of thoughts enables you to answer.

You have been a hope of metamorphosis. The volcano of life leaves ashes to hopeless but the before instilled moments keep you going

Revenge

Revenge is like a mirror. Only when fully broken does the shattered pieces of glass reflect, the pain which was fully caused. Pain is pain; no matter what angle it is looked at from. To seek revenge means often times inner injury is left.

Different thought processes, generate different results. When someone, take you out of your mental cage by first showing you the mirror of what could be and then let that mirror break. It is then that the shattered glass glisten. The broken glass are the people, who give you the splinters which occur only when damage is already done, with its sharp edges.

You want the person who inflicted this scatted nest to know how you feel...sorry does not unravel the movements interject into your being. Events rewinding itself again and again.

To live is to learn. In doing so self-control must first take place. Revenge is the speed but gravity which is the peace need to keep calm.

Riveting

Knowing is simple. Bidding for satisfaction is not always doable. Your character has been riveting. Gaining access to someone so in depth with goals reachable has been game changing.

To address high mental mountains is difficult. creating a forecast of greatness rarely occurs. Grab opportunities like a magnetic force to form a complete element.

Riveting yes-you are very much so. You are the tarmac which is needed to authorize building the road. You start of soft but then finish of hard with signs.

Cars run on that road with engines awaiting drivers to-hurry along the process. One car stops ever so often, to peep close by the window at the front. Shuttered glass near the back waiting to be cleaned. It will need a spray but firstly closure of protection from the riveting road must be mobile.

The end

Printed in Great Britain
by Amazon

28854827R10030